This is What was Next

poems by

Emily McKay

Finishing Line Press
Georgetown, Kentucky

This is What was Next

Copyright © 2020 by Emily McKay
ISBN 978-1-64662-348-8 First Edition
All rights reserved under International and Pan-American Copyright Conventions. No part of this book may be reproduced in any manner whatsoever without written permission from the publisher, except in the case of brief quotations embodied in critical articles and reviews.

ACKNOWLEDGMENTS

I would like to thank the literary magazines and journals that first published several poems in this collection, including *Zarf, Vallum, Barrow Street*, and *Subjectiv*.

I was also fortunate enough to study Creative Writing at the University of Saint Andrews with writers John Burnside, Don Paterson, Lesley Glaister, Meaghan Delahunt, and Jacob Polley, whose invaluable insights and encouragement will always stay with me.

Publisher: Leah Huete de Maines
Editor: Christen Kincaid
Cover Art: Zsofia Penzvalto
Author Photo: Emily McKay
Cover Design: Elizabeth Maines McCleavy

Order online: www.finishinglinepress.com
also available on amazon.com

Author inquiries and mail orders:
Finishing Line Press
P. O. Box 1626
Georgetown, Kentucky 40324
U. S. A.

Table of Contents

Come in and Explore the Bibliophobe's Paradise! 1

For a Sign 2

Between Hosts 4

Bycatch 5

Backtrack 7

Waltz 8

Earth or Water, Fire or Air 9

Eucharist, Super 11

Acclimb 12

yin-yang 13

What Comes Down, Must 14

On the Impossibility of Existential Bulimia 15

Outage in the Swamps 16

Property Seizure 18

Here's to Them 19

All the Unaltered Toms 20

From the Nightstand 21

so and so 22

The Promise, Outbroken 25

Come in and Explore the Bibliophobe's Paradise!

Leave the living stones
firm and balanced in the wall
    good as tall and wide
Do not gather the chips
or symbols of the obelisk
    good as hard and heavy
or probe the columbarium
with questions it hears all day
    good as first and full
What do you want to know?
you are not in those pages
    good as light and free
If good stones are stones that elicit emotion
all stones are good to us
    good as cold and sweaty
but from here your form is biggest
in the cave (so keep close)
    good as bones and butter

For a Sign

(it will talk to you off the record
like I'm talking to you now)

A large red tweed envelope
sealed with buttermilk frosting and stamped by the ancient signet ring
that harks from the top of the tower of Babel
is traveling through the post,
addressed to the whole of your stomach

(it will talk to you transitively,
contextualizing, prefacing, clearing the stage for)

but it must touch you
when you're looking the other way
before you can read it

(it will talk to you constantly, rapidly, vapidly,
uncrystalizing your semantic maps, draining your ulcerated cosmology
until you are both struck anonymous
again
and deeper
at every refrain)

and its distance from you
         broken pencil mangling the writing on the wall
    will day by day
         ambiguous dew on the fleece, night after night
    acquire dimensions

(it will give you nothing
if it will not exist)

          so you must press to your tongue
          the black and blue beequilts inside all the empty envelopes
          and your tongue must salivate generously,
          must lie prostrate before the right honorable flavor

        you must paint from memory
        the postmarks of Christmas cards pastpresent&future
        and the price of their journeys
        your breath must harmonize with the cricketclicks of dusk
        and answer the Morse riddles of winking stars
        as fingerless prints tuck you into bed

        and in the morning you will learn that you have learned
        how to digest the cardboard, glue, and ink
    already so kindly leatherbound and signed
    already given and ground and lined
by unwhomsoever
beside your sugar pills.

Between Hosts

A pair of water moccasins mark the way to Sheol
in the hollows between cypress roots
on the bank of the river's source;
the cottonmouth aligns itself scale by scale
to the wry elbows, wrists,
and calloused heels
of the willow branch,
swooping over the water
like an expanding lower lip.

Spotted hemlock, nightshade, and the ivies
weave networks of poison
on their loom of seedlings' necks;
tight soiree of stems ever prying,
strangling giants for one petal of sun,
cracking ribs just to see inside,
their sunrise blooms green after green.

Their leaves are embroidered with ticks, lone stars
on their journeys between hosts;
a hundred raccoons in hundreds more shadows
wring black rainbows out of feathers at the bank,
but those remain unkissed
who already foam, or stumble.

Bycatch

Sheets of crimped mesh purse together into the great fractal
overhead, which is realized more than seen
    it is here
    sinking in
and known, not by the ringing of hundreds of taut cables,
but a thunder so close
one is as good as struck.
    we are not the ones
    we are the wrong ones
One incidental ribbon of eel, stunned limp beneath the avalanche
of precious metals tumbling from their own worth,
is in love, for a short and shining now, with such oneness,
such spacelessness, such tight self,
but is soon muscled out through a secret door
by the unsmothered
fighting itself
to the death.
The eel, still not itself and profoundly none other,
follows the teardrop haul through the open
    I don't know how long
    I don't know how far
concealed only by the shadow-cloud of scales erupting like shook
dust, cloud rolling swollen with puffs of bluing blood and raining
petals of gill, cloud spinning electric with swarms of shards of eye,
their sacred shape ground beneath unthinkable black weight
how the glitter flies, almost in synchrony
    it is sinking in
    is it pain
    we ask you with our hive of eyes
        I do not know things
        I do everything but know it
Choreography slides off their bodies and converges at the tips of
their fins, and then never was. Their hearts continue to beat only
as a formal statement of nerves, until both chambers agree
that time cannot be kept. Synapses lose their grip.
silent beasts must come and go

in silence the eel wakes
alone in the wide arena of dusk
just able to make out the pendulum disappearing toward the
shallow water of the golden city where it is received by a huge swarm
of square mammalian teeth, riding, if they please, upon pink lips
that undulate through the water like nudibranchs, squeezing into
every pore of coral, every cave, into the tightest of schools and shoals,
gnashing and grinding and grating and chattering mechanically
as they pace and race up the seabed, scattered mobs of them
fighting and cramming into the most coveted lips

But, more than just remarkable invertebrates, they say things
and they know things and they feel things and they say
they know they feel pain but they are too fast
and unhungry to fight or understand
                      we answer only by seeing

Backtrack

strawberries roll
across the kitchen floor
she has heard this bounce before
could be her ears or lips or hands or knees
could be a street or a bed or a wall or a door

bruises lift like mountains on a treasure map
leading to Night, to the night before—
a skipping stone stitching the moon
from lip-to-lipsticked rim,
its trail diving, dissolving
in the arms of bubbles
in the effervescence
of a lost string
of pearls

Waltz

I kissed you from the left, after
you debunked the afterlife;
she kissed me from the left, as if to neutralize

you were warned by text of horsemen,
you were warned by text of flames;
she begged me to drown with her but

she found the sea too cold.
you saw and you believed when
she slid Virginia Woolf under the door

over and over again.

Earth or Water, Fire or Air

Day is but sun, day is but one seamless sunaftersun
but still I wake to it, wake with a start to it
as if for the first time, wake to my breaking
breaking into smaller, eversmaller, evensmaller
pieces of the mountains I once so proudly carved.
Until the year, at last the year, after an eternity of stinging drought,
this is the year of the monsoon.

I hear the beat and roar of your army on the horizon,
flashing the teeth you tore from the sun
as you fill the sky
bellowing with a voice too deep for any mortal mouth
as you darken the earth
swelling toward that world which knows you
as the oasis braces myself

at last the wind sweeps the sand off my endless hunched shoulders
and sends shivers down my endless ridgeback dunes, at last, at last,
at last you lean down from the crackling black to meet me again,
again with a brush and a hum and a kiss of rain for every grain of sand,
again draw out this crumbling skeleton with the old flood
that explodes with the lifeblood of lazuli, white velvet, and down,
and erase this place where I wait,
replace its desperate mirages:
The ends of time are retying.

The cold wind you stole from the sea
plunges and circles and swarms before
the outpour, night of nights, finally breaks;
all the seeds of my grasses, all the eggs of my beetles
hidden long, hidden deep, now stir,
every hollow of me an open mouth

but as your rain falls,
such is the scream of my heat
such is the vacuum of my aridity

that all your gifts are halted   midair
all your tenderness   evaporates
back up to you
slowly   heavy   great directionless vapor
you cannot touch me
and without you, you never will

so gather your robes and cross our stars as you go
and you must, must go, go west, must west or east or north or south,
you are all ways and all-going and must always go, go to love the living

all my endless mouths gape on
from the breath you stole away,
that thinnest and last puff of moisture,
that last glint of anything, born away
from my all endless my splitting lips

Eucharist, Super

O beard-netted deli man,
O plexiglass donut dollhouse
O tank of rubbercuffed lobsters
O semireflective office windows of the HR tabernacle, built o'er
the motion sensor city gate

no hero can exist here, no history in any aisle;
gravity a trapped sparrow that dares not land

O God you are a God
without administrative cherubim
O God you are a God
wholly consumed by data entry
O God you are a God
struggling to file this huge polystyrene omniscience

At night we sparrows descend
the tree of knowledge neither good nor evil
and we queue
and we know

whether we're lions or bureaucrats or art teachers,
whether I have mushrooms or gold or kittens,
it's one dream, and I'd be missing the point
to ask what you mean, or your beard, or your meat

Acclimb

The bulb   at the bottom of the stairs explodes and
I cannot hear   where shards if shards have landed
in the birchbark dark   of the first night in the house,
but crystal grains of pollen   must be cozying between
each blade of carpet, and crescent moons   floating down to each
pleat of the horizon, while maple seeds spin alone, even now.

It is   evening now, but I am not intoxicated
because   spirits are hidden in this country.
They are not sold   by or beside the juniper trees
or by star anise, or   by mint. They do not flow
through the aquifer, or   ascend from wells, or
hang under ferns in the morning.   But I feel the same
untrustworthy tingling, that lightness   and looseness of
nerves; I am snowflakes without bones,   without joints,
who can pick their feet up again, who pick   their feet up
again just to fall from somewhere newer than the sky.

I do not know   how many stairs if stairs in this
velvet arcticky dark of the   first night in the house
but I take two at a time, and fast   maybe three, maybe
four because of the invisible leopard   haunches and
invisible foxspring of my invisible body in my invisible   life
 in this sublime and ineffable dark of the first night in the house.

yin-yang

The perfect dot of island on the lake
and its single peridot apple tree
were too idyllic not to swim to.
The further I went,
the further it was
but I was already halfway—
so what was I to do
when the giant snapper
I hadn't believed in
raised its thorny nostrils up out of the water
and turned

What Comes Down, Must

Theses decompose themselves
as soon as the last cardboard box is sealed,
its corners all that's left to contest
the echoes of the empty flat.

I could make out the burnt knot
of eucalyptus and the ink that still seemed to bubble
across the flexed pages of John Donne,
except those love poems from his sticky younger years
already smoked in cheeky protest,
coiled rounding glowing leaves.
Passing our glow between us
like a telescope fixed on Mars,
our world was black and white
and black and white, it blazed here,
then boiled to a kind of resin, tricky
but brittle now, and easy to sweep
off the brick.

Not a working fireplace,
lied the landlord,
twelve months ago tomorrow.

On the Impossibility of Existential Bulimia

The elders tried to bribe my sister with candy
to make her smile
when she was five; I thought five
was the happiest age when I was six,
and our sevens we ate separately,
in the privacy of our own years.
You have to eat the whole thing.
You have to eat the whole thing.
Eight, nine, they keep filling up, filling up faster
than our plates could brace themselves, faster
than our forks and knives could cut them into days

A decade later she broke a sob in a restaurant
—just a single freak flash—
before she straightened her silverware intently
and lowered her voice:
  starvation was my only sense of power.
  no one else could do it.
  and no one else could be silent either.
And with that, flat and plain,
she snapped a leaf off the centerpiece
and rolled it between two fingers
until she'd pinched it to a spitty pulp:
  I hate
  god I hate
  birthday cake.

Outage in the Swamps

tiny shadows swirl across the warping trailer floor
cast by the heatwaves drooling at the window—
how they pinwheel, how they swim
through the sparkling nebulous dust
like tea leaves steeping;
pipesmoke, a drop of milk.

beyond the sweatstains, beyond the mire,
beyond the heartbeat, beyond the bloodheat,
and any scent of me, I zero
beyond the magmatic breakshapes
widening between me and the social animals,
beyond the span
of
a pennydrop,

daylight is striped, the sun is folded blind
as it passes through my window;
beams hang suspended in the moltengold
like yellow boas poising for a better view –

rusty light, creaky light strains and grunts its way
into the perfect meshape in the couch
where my skull falls back maybe too far,
falls beyond the bloodstains,
falls beyond the mold,
falls beyond the heartbreak,
and any span of me

rickety light, arthritic light, light burnt and bruised
paints bandages of shade across my chest—
here, shivers, shivers, here? a bliss that cannot be
like the snake charmer's melody
cannot be remembered out of the dream

and at last a thorn
a monster of burning thorn,
which would have been so painful
if I had noticed it before,
is pulled from the center
of my sternum,
lifting the pain cleanly out of
everywhere,
everywhereintheworldeverywhere
and it shoots through the ceiling
like a cooped-up bullet
who will need his mother
only after he gets through his juice boxes
and bags of pretzels.

Property Seizure

As soon as I move, I remember
the hundreds of seashells in bed with me,
none of them the kind
you should put your ear to.

The lemon twist you left
at the bottom of the gin
begins to grow legs, gills,
then lungs and discontent;
housedust gathers on the sea,
rain on the windowsill.

I no longer know
though maybe you do
which are pillboxes, which are plates,
or which landmarks of the house
will erode as soon
as my eyes rest upon them,
so that my eyes may never rest

though maybe yours do.
So I keep fixed to the backs of my retinas
petroglyphs of togetherness:
curling lighthouse bricks, and wool,
and the scales of schools of fish
to plant in lucid dreams
of a still life.

Here's to Them

my heart is burning like trees
the alder is bending like children are pulling its leaves
only every other leaf
here's to hoping

the fox sees her whiskers beginning to curl
but surely the source will pull back and inhale
this is nothing to her, just whiskers curling, just whiskers
here's to hoping

fur is crisping deep in the burrow
and the roots of Spring cringe brown
only every other burrow
only every other Spring
here's to hoping

the deer are scanning for the source of the roar:
the thicket is not, nor the treetops
the meadow is not, nor the muddy pond,
but the valley, in the valley,
the deer are scanning the valley,
flash after flash, chimneys stand tall
while houses go up in smoke
Every tree is burning.
Every tree is burning.

All the Unaltered Toms

Shocking but also hardly, the Panhandle
tires of drowning its unwanted litters,
so instead it throws them out pickup windows
like bottles, tumbling 50 mph,
unravelling all evidence of themselves

When I first saw these scraps of fur on the highway,
blackening like grease forgotten on the skillet,
I drove round round round so excited
to be the savior of something
before, I assumed, it toddled blindly across the road

So when somebody told me, no one dared tell me
that life was sacred in Florida
while unopened eyes spin out in a single arc through the night
like a whole sky of shooting stars
when NASCAR's on TV.

From the Nightstand

Green stem of incense burns auroral, burns grey
while its smoke splits into two stiles of a ladder
and as it climbs itself to unknowable heights,
ghosts across the city unfurl from chimneys
like lilies, to the warm swirling currents
where vultures soar and sleep;
each silver cord wrung
uniquely.

so and so

bethany brethaway was the name she signed
and tucked under the riverstones that no one overturned,
aging poorly against the current;
was the name she built with unstruck flint and steel,
was the name she scratched out and rubbed
until the canvas was felted raw,
and the felt lifted up her paintings' foggy scribble-lined clouds;
was the name that bled out in spurts and in longlong winelegs
down the fingerbones of Autumn leaves,
shrinking immediately to the color of dried blood,
wintering before they ever knew the gold paint of Spring
   —because it is very expensive and hard to come by.

evelyn peregrine hung up all her nameplaces
in the painterwage boathouse
tethered to the grey granite walls of the canal;
       these walls, so says The Painter
in the upscale boathouse downstream,
       are not grey but silver;
and yes, she did concede, on a bright day,
when the breeze mistakes the rough rock for a saltlick as it flies by,
it tends to leave a little glitter;

the silver paint she could not afford she tried to mine
from the beams of windowlight sometimes trapped, as if it a web,
against the surface of the murk where she swirled her brushes clean,
where she stirred and stirred but only ever stirred
the rainbow of all her paints
back into their blunt charcoal sky.

adelaide dalloway knocked on The Painter's door
to ask for a drop of aqua
but before she could pass through the threshold,
he pulled up a chair and ordered her
       SIT:
bringing her face to face with his freshestframed work.

He studied her study it and to his delight,
it took her breath away—
she didn't know if it was beautiful or compelling or clever
or whatever it is that pleases Those Men pleased by paintings,
but within the grids and sparks of color,
she found her precious aqua, exactly as she'd dreamt,
cradled in tiny rectangles of bronze, bronze that really did glitter,
bronze lathered in generous strokes,
strokes thick as throbbing arteries,
strokes sure as rolling lava kneading itself
from red to black and steaming
strokes voluptuous as Renaissance nudes sprawling across
the world's finest silks and furs from the gentlest living looms;
and aqua pooling blue blue oh blue
aqua like lakes resting windless in the craters of ancient volcanoes,
aqua like a rainbalm easing the scars of a star's lucky strike
aqua like oh god it's a portrait, oh god it's of me

marianna carrigan feared to paint or be painted a lie,
so if ever a hair of her brush strayed from The Real
      wait! coos the Moss from the belly of the boat,
      we must wait
      for The Real to be good wheneverifever that be;
      we must be the dream within the wake
because within a dream within the dream, we will be
worst or best, at best, in a dreamworld, only by dreamrules—
so meanwhile she tacked canvas by canvas by day and by night
row after row round her walls, like sharks' teeth lining the jaw
like an endless fan of cards,
like a closing rose,
save one little square
of window

      If you want to be good,
so say the Crayfish in the shadows of the Minnows in the shallows,
      if you want to win,

   you must be like everybody else.
   If the world paints flowers, don't you dare
   give them geometry or troubled dreams.
   Give them one stamen of diamond, just one
   no matter what petals you have.
But bethany brethaway's troubled dreams
were Flowers

so says The Painter:
   That beauty that pleases Those Men pleased by paintings,
   is the Holy Grail, however Beautiful the Grail is or is not
   So you Must Ever And EVer,
   FORever ENDEavor TO
   PLEASE ALL MEN
   amen

so they say,
so and so,
so they say.

The Promise, Outbroken

I never heard any murmurs,
never saw any low brows or sideways glances
of anyone who would cut the wires or crack the glass,
unlock the gates or the hatches,
or spin open the padlock of the sepulcher

Most of us held back in our warm, dry confessionals
though all of our doors were opened;
the lorikeets and ocelots and shrews fared well
as did the adders, jackals, and eagles
while the camels backed themselves into a corner
and the baboons were lured in with apples,
and the lion
lumbered, so tired,
across the street
to a golf course,
collapsed in a sunny patch of green,
and felt the hemispheres of his brain sigh and slouch
against the walls of his skull.
Warming, rewarding themselves,
absorbing the tranquility
shot from the tranquility gun;
oh heavy head, uncradled, thunderstruck, undone
but for the blurry rain of roses thrown across the whole of his mind—
red for passion, for rapture, for rupture, for love,
then white.

But I, dull brown female specimen
of the paradise birds, perch unseen
in a tree with the pigeons in the park.
No stones thrown now, or bread,
no one to notate my behavior,
no plaques to explain my favorite corner.
This is what was next:
the space,
the spaces,
the nestlessness,
the burning muscles of birds
flying inscrutably
towards

Emily McKay is a Creative Writing MLitt graduate of the University of Saint Andrews, UK, where she also earned an undergraduate MA in English & Philosophy. In the seven years since, she has found herself working as a cheesemonger in Scotland, veterinary receptionist in Florida, an electrical calibration technician in California, and now an electro-optical test engineer in the Seattle area, where she lives with her husband, three feline muses, and old rabbit Stewart.

Her poetry and short stories have appeared in *Glimmer Train, Shenandoah, Vallum, Barrow Street, The Conium Review, Fugue, Flock, Zarf,* and *Subjectiv.* Along with ongoing poetry projects, she is currently working on a book-length compilation of found text and an extended personal essay on the nature of mourning animals.

www.ingramcontent.com/pod-product-compliance
Lightning Source LLC
LaVergne TN
LVHW041520070426
835507LV00012B/1718